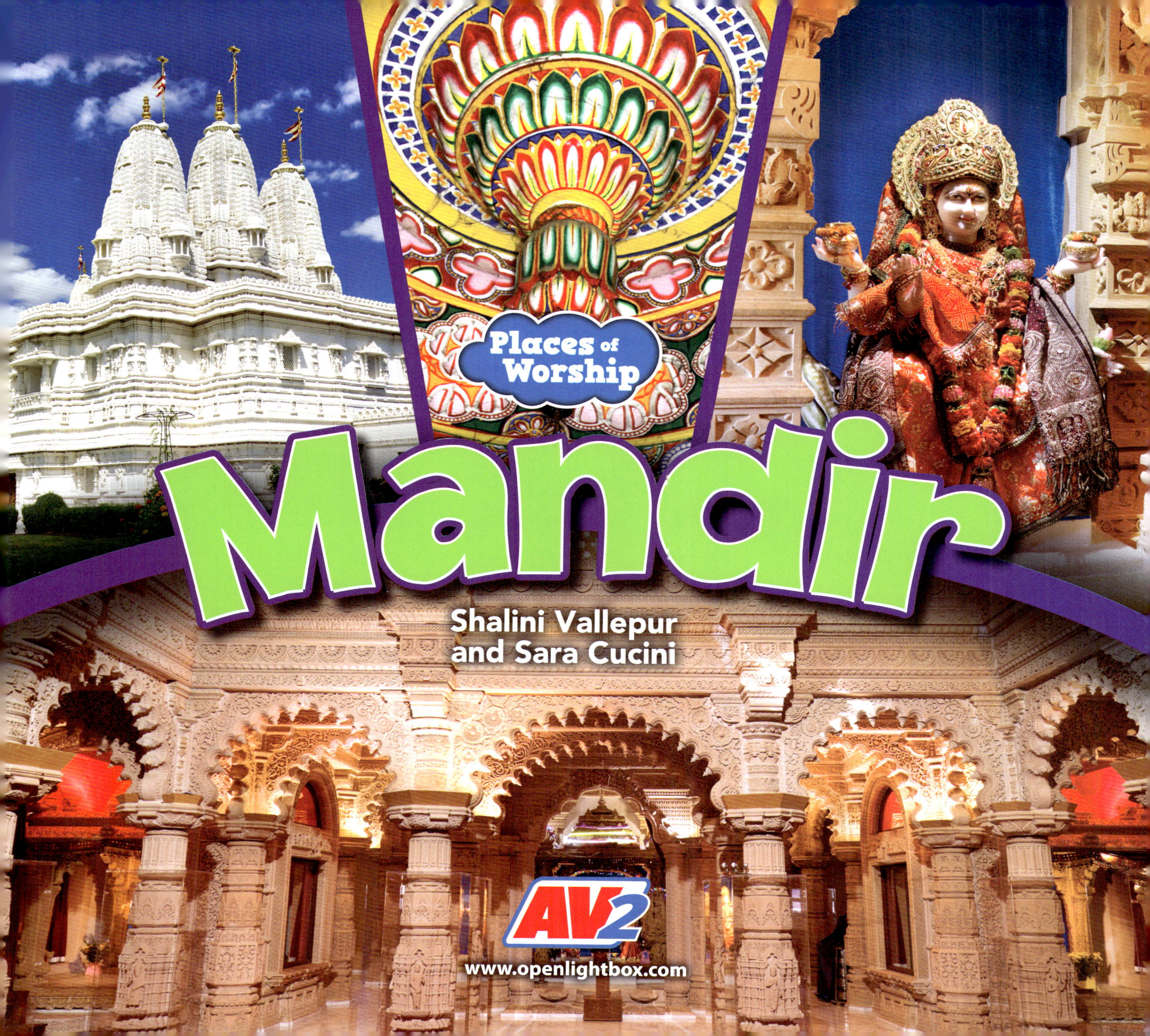
Places of Worship
Mandir
Shalini Vallepur
and Sara Cucini
AV2
www.openlightbox.com

Step 1
Go to **www.openlightbox.com**

Step 2
Enter this unique code
VNBREYOQ3

Step 3
Explore your interactive eBook!

Places of Worship
Mandir
Start!
Share

AV2 is optimized for use on any device

Your interactive eBook comes with...

Audio
Listen to the entire book read aloud

Videos
Watch informative video clips

Weblinks
Gain additional information for research

Try This!
Complete activities and hands-on experiments

Key Words
Study vocabulary, and complete a matching word activity

Quizzes
Test your knowledge

Slideshows
View images and captions

Share
Share titles within your Learning Management System (LMS) or Library Circulation System

Citation
Create bibliographical references following APA, CMOS, and MLA styles

This title is part of our AV2 digital subscription

1-Year K–5 Subscription
ISBN 978-1-7911-3320-7

Access hundreds of AV2 titles with our digital subscription.
Sign up for a FREE trial at **www.openlightbox.com/trial**

The digital components of this book are guaranteed to stay active for at least five years from the date of publication.

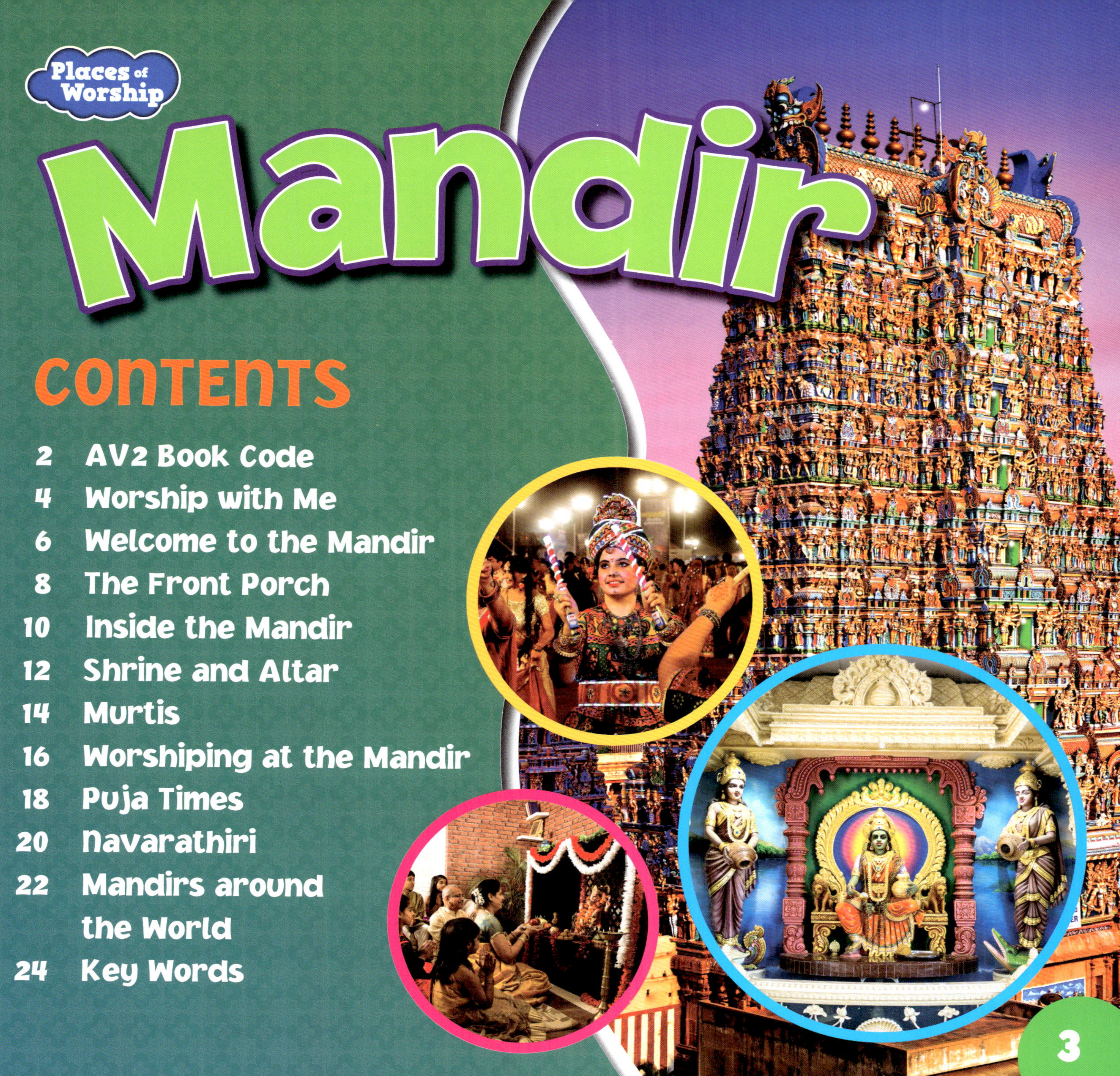

Places of Worship

Mandir

CONTENTS

2 AV2 Book Code
4 Worship with Me
6 Welcome to the Mandir
8 The Front Porch
10 Inside the Mandir
12 Shrine and Altar
14 Murtis
16 Worshiping at the Mandir
18 Puja Times
20 Navarathiri
22 Mandirs around the World
24 Key Words

Worship with Me

Have you ever been to a mandir? A mandir is a building of worship for followers of **Hinduism**, who are called **Hindus**.

Hinduism began in **India** more than **4,000** years ago.

Hindus believe in many gods and goddesses. People called **Pujaris** carry out rituals at the mandir to honor these gods and goddesses.

Welcome to the Mandir

Mandirs all over the world can look very different from each other. Some mandirs have one tower, known as a **shikhara**. Others have many towers.

The main area of worship is usually underneath the mandir's biggest **dome**.

Many mandirs have a **flag** outside. These flags are usually orange. Some have the symbols of different gods on them.

Main Hindu Gods and Goddesses

The Trimurti

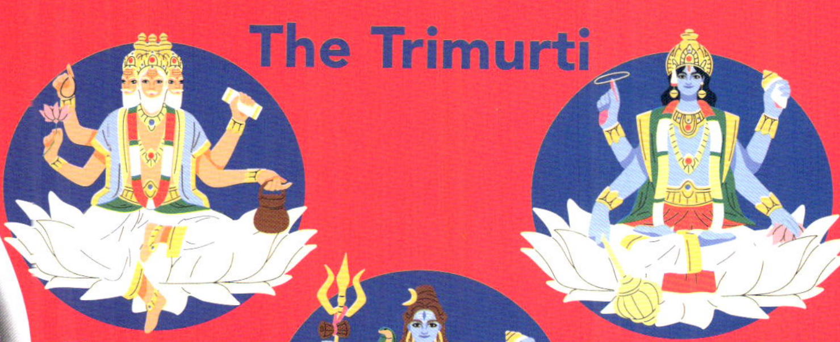

Brahma

Vishnu

Shiva

The Tridevi

Lakshmi

Parvati

Saraswati

The Front Porch

It is important to be clean before entering a mandir. Some mandirs have a porch outside where people can **wash** their **feet**.

Many mandirs have a big **bell** or bells at the **entrance**. Worshipers ring the bell when they go in and out of the mandir.

A mandir's bell is called a **ghanta**. It can be made from a mixture of different metals, including **copper**, **zinc**, **silver**, **gold**, and **iron**.

Inside the Mandir

People usually wear clothes that cover their **arms** and **legs** when they go to the mandir. When entering a mandir, people must also take off their **shoes**.

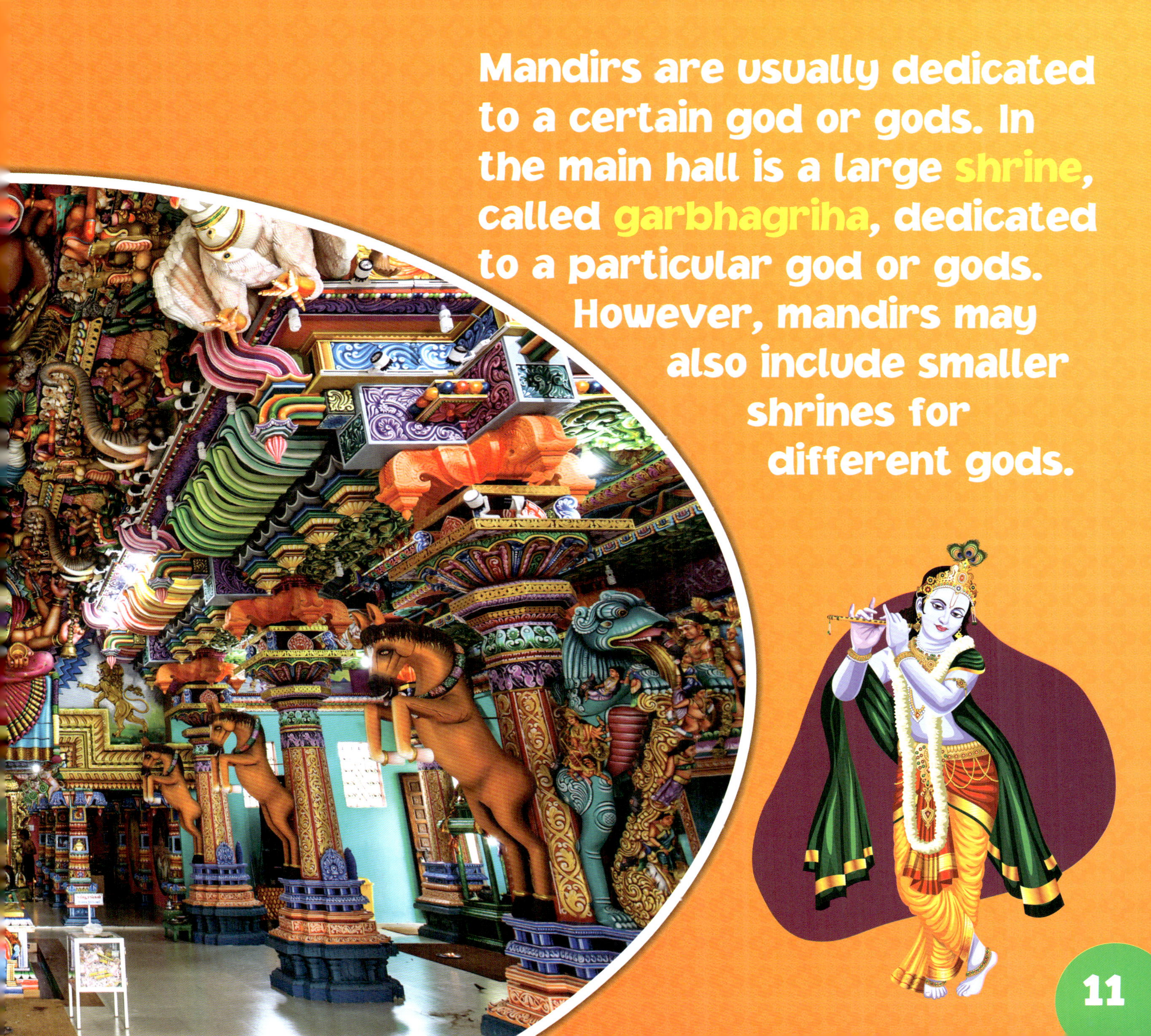

Mandirs are usually dedicated to a certain god or gods. In the main hall is a large **shrine**, called **garbhagriha**, dedicated to a particular god or gods. However, mandirs may also include smaller shrines for different gods.

Shrine and Altar

There is an altar at most shrines. Most altars have a bell, incense, and lamps.

A **food offering** of rice, fruit, or butter is sometimes made during worship. This is called **Prasada**. The food is brought to the altar on a special plate. Then, it is blessed and given to the god.

Prasada
Altar
Lamp
Bell
Incense

Murtis

Shrines usually have one **murti**. Murtis are **statues** of the gods and goddesses. Worshipers try to visit all the shrines and murtis in the mandir.

The garbhagriha may be surrounded by walls. In some mandirs, only the Pujaris are allowed near murtis. When the worshipers reach the garbhagriha, they walk around it.

Worshiping at the Mandir

Hindu worship is called **puja**. During puja, worshipers sit in front of the garbhagriha.

Pujaris chant mantras in **Sanskrit** in front of the shrine. They wave a lamp around the shrine, the murti, and the worshipers. This is called **aarti**.

Shiva Mantras

Shiva is one of the best-known Hindu gods. He is believed to be the god who destroys the universe so it can be recreated. There are many mantras dedicated to Shiva. This is one of them.

ॐ
नमः
शिवाय

Om Namah Shivaya

(Pronunciation
Ohm na-maah shee-vah-yuh)

"I bow to Shiva."

Puja Times

There are no set times for puja, but it usually happens around sunrise, midday, sunset, and midnight at the mandir.

Many Hindus also worship at **home**. They may have a small shrine in their homes with their own murtis, bells, and incense.

Navarathiri

Navarathiri is a nine-day festival that celebrates when the Goddess **Durga** defeated the demon **Mahishasura**.

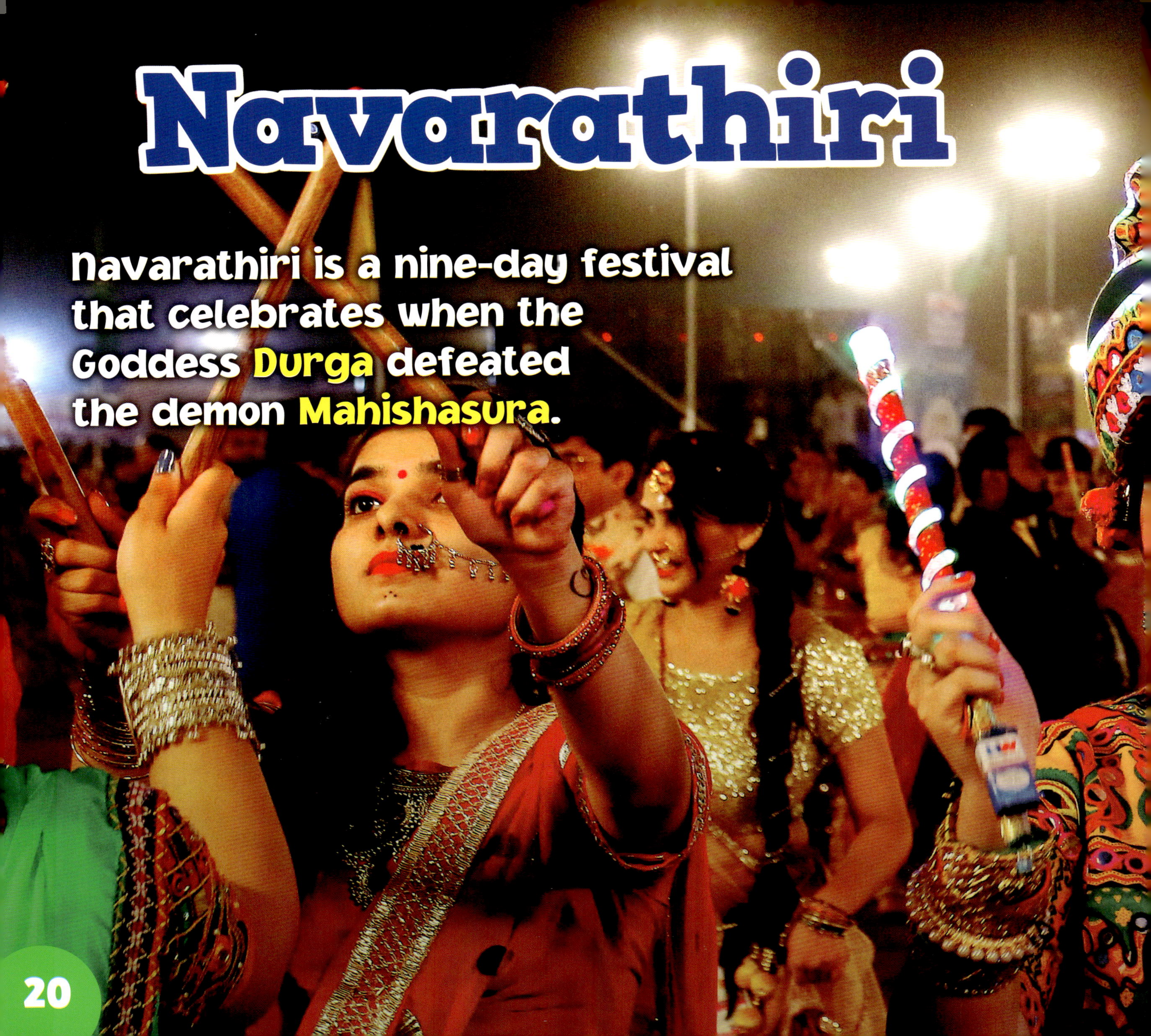

Little statues called golu are placed in some mandirs. Many people celebrate by doing a dance called Dandiya with special sticks.

Durga is usually represented with several arms and riding a lion or tiger.

Mandirs around the World

Meenakshi Amman Temple

Madurai, India

Tanath Lot

Bali, Indonesia

Banteay Srei
Angkor Archaeological Site, Cambodia

BAPS Shri Swaminarayan Mandir
Houston, Texas, United States

KEY WORDS

Research has shown that as much as 65 percent of all written material published in English is made up of 300 words. These 300 words cannot be taught using pictures or learned by sounding them out. They must be recognized by sight. This book contains 82 common sight words to help young readers improve their reading fluency and comprehension. This book also teaches young readers several important content words, such as proper nouns.

Page	Sight Words First Appearance
4	a, are, been, began, for, have, in, is, me, more, of, than, to, who, with, years, you
5	and, at, carry, many, out, people, the, these
6	all, as, can, different, from, look, one, others, over, some, very, world
7	on, them
8	be, before, feet, important, it, their, where
9	big, go, made, or, they, when
10	also, must, off, take, that
11	large, may
12	an, food, most, sometimes, then, there, this
14	try
15	around, by, near, only, walk
17	he, so
18	but, no, set, times
19	home, own
20	day
21	little

Page	Content Words First Appearance
4	building, followers, Hinduism, Hindus, India, mandir, worship
5	goddesses, gods, Pujaris, rituals
6	area, dome, shikhara, tower
7	Brahma, flag, Lakshmi, Parvati, Saraswati, Shiva, symbols, Tridevi, Trimurti, Vishnu
8	porch
9	bell, copper, entrance, ghanta, gold, iron, metals, mixture, silver, zinc
10	arms, clothes, legs, shoes
11	garbhagriha, hall, shrine
12	altar, butter, fruit, incense, lamps, offering, plate, Prasada, rice
14	murtis, statues
15	walls
16	aarti, mantras, puja, Sanskrit
17	pronunciation, universe
18	midday, midnight, sunrise, sunset
20	demon, Durga, festival, Mahishasura, Navarathiri
21	dance, Dandiya, golu, lion, sticks, tiger

Published by Lightbox Learning Inc.
276 5th Avenue, Suite 704 #917
New York, NY 10001
Website: www.openlightbox.com

Library of Congress Control Number: 2024935502

ISBN 978-1-5105-8189-0 (hardcover)
ISBN 979-8-8745-1511-9 (softcover)
ISBN 978-1-5105-8190-6 (static multi-user eBook)
ISBN 978-1-5105-8192-0 (interactive multi-user eBook)

Printed in Guangzhou, China
1 2 3 4 5 6 7 8 9 0 28 27 26 25 24

052024
100923

Project Coordinator: Sara Cucini
Designer: Jean Faye Rodriguez

Every reasonable effort has been made to trace ownership and to obtain permission to reprint copyright material. The publisher would be pleased to have any errors or omissions brought to its attention so that they may be corrected in subsequent printings.

The publisher acknowledges Getty Images, Alamy, and Shutterstock as the primary image suppliers for this title.

First published by BookLife in 2020.